c

WINNING

POKER

Published by

Black Dog & Leventhal Publishers, Inc.
151 West 19th Street
New York, NY 10011

Distributed by

Workman Publishing Company
708 Broadway
New York, NY 10003

Manufactured in China

Cover and interior design by 27.12 Design, Ltd.
ISBN: 1-57912-403-8
g f e d c b

Library of Congress Cataloging-in-Publication Data is on file
at Black Dog & Leventhal Publishers, Inc.

WINNING

POKER

200 Rules, Techniques & Strategies

DEAN MATTHEWSON & ANGIE DiAMOND

BLACK DOG
& LEVENTHAL
PUBLISHERS
NEW YORK

CONTENTS

PART 1: THE BASICS

PART 2: THE GAMES

PART 3:
USING THE NUMBERS AND YOUR NOGGIN   83

PART 4: OTHER VENUES AND RESOURCES   99

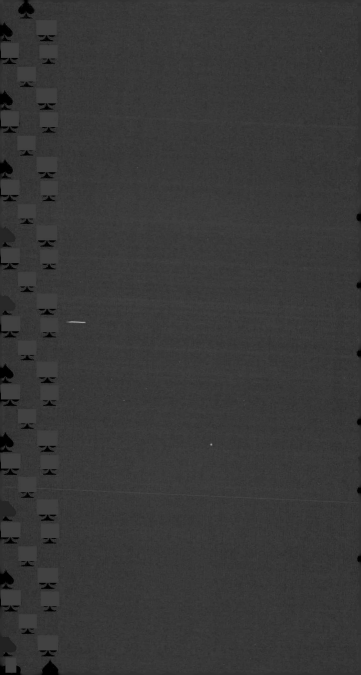

PART 1
THE BASICS

What You Need to Play

- **DECK OF FIFTY-TWO CARDS**

  It would hardly be poker without the cards. If you are playing with a brand-new deck, take out the Jokers and any miscellaneous cards, and then give the deck a good shuffle. If you are playing with a used deck, make sure it is complete and inspect the cards for any wear-and-tear that may "mark" them. It's a good idea to have more than one deck in case one gets damaged. Also, as one player is dealing a hand, the player to his right should prepare the other deck for the next game.

- **POKER CHIPS**

  Real clay poker chips are expensive and more of a luxury than a necessity. Plastic chips will do just fine. However, these inexpensive sets usually have only three different colored chips. If you want more value-levels of chips, then you may need to go to a specialty store.

- **A GOOD TABLE WITH AMPLE ROOM**

- **SNACKS & BEVERAGES**

  (optional, but recommended)
  No one likes to lose, and no one likes to lose on an empty stomach, so keep some snacks around (nothing too messy). Note: Most professional players would never risk impairing their judgment by drinking alcohol while playing.

What You Need to Decide

- **VALUE OF POKER CHIPS**
  You can assign any value you choose to the chips. However, the colors usually correspond to a particular value sequence. For instance, in a regular set, the white chips correspond to the lowest value, the reds are in the middle, and the blue chips are worth the most. Sometimes there are also green, black, or purple chips. If you want to play for higher stakes you can go to the next level and play with green, black, and purple chips; purple is the king of chips.

- **MINIMUM/MAXIMUM BETS & NUMBER OF RAISES**
  In order to keep "friendly" games friendly, it is best to set the betting amounts before you begin. For instance, if your lowest chip is worth ten cents, then the opening minimum bet can be set at ten cents. Depending on how much money you are playing with, a maximum bet can also be established. Before you begin play, you should also decide how many raises per player will be allowed during each hand.

- **ANTE**
  The ante is the amount that all players add to the pot before each game begins. It should be determined before you sit down to play. Commonly, whatever your lowest chip value is determines the ante. Some people have the dealer ante for everyone at the beginning of each hand; this prevents the confusion that sometimes ensues when someone forgets to ante.

Ranking of Hands:
THE BACKBONE OF POKER

Learning the ranking of hands is essential. Make sure you know what beats what before you start playing. Hands are listed in descending order from strongest to weakest:

- **ROYAL FLUSH**

  The five highest cards in sequence, all of the same suit

  EXAMPLE:

  A♣, K♣, Q♣, J♣, 10♣

  TIES: Two or more Royal Flushes split the pot.

- **STRAIGHT FLUSH**

  Five consecutive cards, all of the same suit, but not a Royal Straight Flush

  EXAMPLE:

  6♥, 5♥, 4♥, 3♥, 2♥

  TIES: Whoever has the highest card in his or her straight wins.

- **FOUR OF A KIND**

  Four cards of the same rank

  EXAMPLE:

  5♣, 5♦, 5♥, 5♠, 10♦

  (The fifth card is irrelevant.)

  TIES: Whoever has the higher-ranking four of a kind wins. (Ex.: Four Jack beats four 10s.)

- **FULL HOUSE**

  Three cards of the same rank plus two cards
  of the same rank

  EXAMPLE:

  K♣, K♥, K♠, 9♥, 9♠

  TIES: Whoever has the higher-ranking three of a
  kind wins.

- **FLUSH**

  Any five cards of the same suit

  EXAMPLE:

  4♦, 5♦, 10♦, K♦, A♦

  TIES: Whoever has a flush with the highest-ranking
  card wins. (If those are the same, compare the
  second-highest cards in the hands, and continue
  down to the fifth card, if necessary.)

- **STRAIGHT**

  Any five cards in sequence

  EXAMPLE:

  7♠, 8♥, 9♥, 10♣, J♦

  TIES: Whoever has the straight with the highest card wins.

- **THREE OF A KIND**

  Three cards of the same rank

  EXAMPLE:

  8♦, 8♥, 8♠, J♥, A♦

  (The other two cards are irrelevant.)

  TIES: The higher-ranking three of a kind wins.
  (Ex.: Three 5s beat three 4s.)

- **TWO PAIR**
  Two different pairs plus an extra card
  EXAMPLE:
  Q♥, Q♠, 10♥, 10♠, 4♦
  TIES: Whoever has the highest-ranking pair wins. (If those cards are the same, the highest-ranking second pair takes it. If still tied, the higher extra card wins.)

- **ONE PAIR**
  Two cards of the same rank plus three extra cards
  EXAMPLE:
  A♦, A♠, 7♣, 6♣, 3♦
  TIES: Whoever has a pair with a higher rank wins. (If the pairs are the same rank, the highest extra card wins.)

- **NO PAIR OR HIGH CARD**
  Any hand that is not at least a pair
  TIES: Whoever has the highest card wins. If the hands are still tied, the second-highest card wins, and so on.

- **THE STATUS OF THE ACE**
  In all games, unless the dealer declares otherwise, Aces are either high or low, but can never go "around the corner" to make a straight (K-A-2-3-4). Obviously, for most hands, you will want the Aces to be high. However, Aces can also be used for low straights (A-2-3-4-5) and as the lowest card in Hi-low games.

The Dealer, Banker & House Rules

- Dealer's Choice or One Game: At the outset of a poker session, players should decide whether to play several games or one game throughout the night. If you play various games, it is the "dealer's choice" as to what game will be played.

- If playing dealer's choice, the dealer decides what game will be played and also if there will be any wild cards.

- The dealer should call out the action as it happens. When dealing a stud game, it is customary to call out what has been dealt, what the potential hands are, and who starts the betting.

- The dealer should keep the game moving. If a player is not paying attention, or is moving too slowly, the dealer can speak up and get the action going again. When it is your turn to deal, don't dawdle – decide your game and deal.

- Think of the dealer as the table's benevolent dicta-tor. It is the dealer's role to know what is going on at all times at the table. The dealer is in charge and can exercise authority by pointing out bad poker etiquette. He or she should feel free to keep players "in line".

- It is in the dealer's (and the game's) best interest to shuffle and to deal carefully. When dealing, never expose the bottom cards or the cards being dealt.

A glimpse at one card can affect the way everyone is playing. Learn how to shuffle discretely. Good shufflers never let the cards leave the table.

- Banker: The group needs to choose a player to be the banker. This person is responsible for collecting money and exchanging it for chips. At the end of the night, or when a player cashes out, the banker collects the chips and doles back whatever each player has earned.

- House Rules: If you are the host and you have particularly strong feelings about certain aspects of poker, then you can declare House Rules. For instance, House Rules might dictate whether Aces are only high for all games or if check-raising is allowed. In addition, House Rules might also be used to establish what rules the dealer needs to address before each hand. The declaration of these guidelines will prevent any disputes over the pot, or any other confusion.

- Final Arbiter: If you are starting out, it's good to keep a book of rules around to settle any disputes – better yet, keep these handy cards around!

Betting:
THE LANGUAGE OF POKER

As many poker players will tell you, poker *is not* gambling; it's a game in which you study the probabilities and make reasonable assumptions based on what's in your hand and on your opponents' cards and behavior. Nevertheless, betting is an integral aspect of poker. Betting is the language through which players convey to the table the strength of their hand. Of course, it is also used to deceive other players, a technique known as bluffing. While each game has its own nuances, there are several aspects common to all games. Before sitting down to play poker, make sure you have a firm knowledge of the basics of betting.

- Ante: This is the agreed-upon amount that all players put into the pot before the hand is dealt. This insures that everyone has at least some stake in winning the hand.

- After the cards have been dealt, the opening player has two options: betting or checking. If he feels confident about his hand, he can start the betting by putting money into the pot. If the opening player is not so confident about his card, he can "check" the bet. Checking means the player is still in, but he is passing the opening bet to the player to his left.

- Once all the other players have made their move, the betting comes back around, and any player who has checked must either "call" or fold (you cannot check twice). (Note: In Omaha and Hold 'em, a player cannot check in the first round of betting.)

- After a player has made a bet, all other players must bet the same amount (also known as "seeing" or "calling"), raise, or fold (quit the hand). If a player raises the bet, he must announce how much he is raising the bet. To stay in, all players must see his raise or fold.

HERE'S HOW A ROUND OF BETTING MIGHT SOUND (IT NEVER HURTS TO KNOW THE LINGO):

- **PLAYER 1:**   Check.
- **PLAYER 2:**   A dollar.
- **PLAYER 3:**   I see your dollar.
- **PLAYER 4:**   Too rich for my blood, I fold.
- **PLAYER 5:**   I see your $1 and raise you $1.
- **PLAYER 1:**   [He must now put in $2 to stay in the game.] I'm in.
- **PLAYER 2:**   [He must now put in $1 to stay in.] I fold.
- **PLAYER 3:**   I'm in.

Types of Players
KNOW THINE ENEMY; KNOW THYSELF

The more poker you play, the better you will become at identifying certain types of players. Though it's no guarantee of complete success, once you have an understanding of how a player approaches the game, you will have gained some much-needed knowledge that will help you read their cards and win some pots. While playing, observe your opponents' style and betting patterns. Things to consider: Do they play slightly recklessly by staying in longer than they should? Are they too conservative and fold immediately if they think they have a bad hand? Do they have the guts to bluff? Keep these things in mind for your own playing as well. It's good to vary your approach—you don't want your opponents to get a handle on you.

- The *loose player* stays in round after round with less-than-perfect hands. In many cases, he is hoping that his hand will improve with new cards. Because he rarely folds, the loose player may win some pots, but by staying in too long, he also loses a lot of pots. After all, the word *loose* looks an awful lot like *lose* and *loser*, doesn't it?

- The *tight player* plays conservatively and gets out early unless he thinks he can win. Tight players rarely chase cards, and they hold on to their money until the time is right and raise bets when confident. If you adopt this style, be careful—it is wise

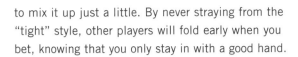

to mix it up just a little. By never straying from the "tight" style, other players will fold early when you bet, knowing that you only stay in with a good hand.

- The *aggressive player,* like the loose player, tends to stay in but is also likely to step up the betting with raises. However, this does not necessarily mean that he or she always has a good hand; the aggressive player may simply enjoy creating some action at the poker table, or he could be bluffing. However, if he does have a good hand, look out— if you stay in, it can cost you some big bucks.

- *Passive players* are less skilled versions of tight players. They don't take risks, fold early, are reluctant to raise, and rarely, if ever, bluff. These players may not feel fully confident of their poker skills, may have already lost some money, or may have simply not discovered the thrill of what gambling is all about.

Poker Etiquette:
MINDING YOUR P'S AND Q'S
(AND YOUR ACES AND KINGS)

A key to enjoying poker (besides winning money) is playing in a game that moves along and is not interrupted by disputes. Here are some tips to insure a smooth game:

- **KNOW THE RULES**

  It is important to learn the rankings of the hands. By constantly referring to a "cheat sheet," you slow down the game. More importantly, you are also essentially telling everyone what's in your hand. For instance, let's say you are playing seven-card stud, and it looks like someone might have a straight and that you may have a flush. If you have to check to see if a flush beats a straight, you might as well announce to your fellow players, "I have a flush; can you beat it?"

- **STATE YOUR INTENTIONS**

  If you are folding, don't just physically fold your cards—declare it. As you see, call, or raise the bet, make sure that you tell the table what you are doing and the amount you are adding to the pot.

- **FOLDING**

  Whenever you fold, never, never show your cards. This gives away valuable information to the remaining players and can seriously affect the course of the hand.

- **YOU REMEMBER THIS ONE FROM KINDERGARTEN**
  Don't gloat and don't be a sore loser.

- **WAIT YOUR TURN**
  It's bad poker etiquette to bet or fold before your turn. Making a move out of turn affects the decisions of the players betting before you. Likewise, if you are holding four Aces and bet out of turn you might be giving away your hand by appearing too eager. In short, hold tight and be patient!

- **DON'T CRITICIZE**
  It displays poor form to criticize or analyze a player's move for the benefit of the table.

- **DON'T LOOK AT YOUR CARDS UNTIL THEY ARE ALL DEALT TO YOU**
  Though there is nothing technically wrong with looking at your cards as they come, in the poker world it's considered uncouth.

- **DO THE CARDS SPEAK OR DO THE PLAYERS?**
  Occasionally, in games with wild cards or games with community cards, a player might misread his hand and actually have a better hand than he declares. For instance, in a seven-card stud game, if deuces are wild and a player is dealt a J, J, 2, 10, 9, 8, 3, he may look at his hand and say, "three Jacks," when in fact, he has a straight (8, 9, 10, J, Q (the 2 acts as a wild card)). So players should decide beforehand if the cards or the players speak.

"For a player to become accepted in a game, knowing how to play poker is not enough. There are accepted forms of behavior at a poker game, some pertaining to the cards and hand being dealt, others pertaining to general house etiquette. You don't stand behind a guy and say, 'Wow! Three Aces!'"

—Stewart Wolpin,
The Rules of Neighborhood Poker According to Hoyle

PART 2

THE GAMES

FIVE-CARD DRAW
The classic

PLAYERS: 3 to 6 is ideal.
CARDS: Five cards, all down.
BETTING: Two rounds plus ante; betting tends to be relatively low.
WHAT TO WATCH FOR: Keep a close eye on how many cards each player draws from the deck.
WHAT WINS: Usually a high pair or better.

Five-card draw, or draw poker, is one of the oldest poker games, and it is unique in that players have the opportunity to exchange their cards or "draw" from the deck to try and improve their hands. So, if you don't like what you see, you can always try your luck with some new cards. Unlike stud games, players only see the cards in their own hands. (But smart players will pay close attention to how many cards other players draw after the first round of betting, as well as their opponents' betting patterns.)

Before opening the game, the dealer must decide how many cards each player can draw from the deck after the first round of betting. The standard limit is three. In some games, a player may draw four cards if he is holding an Ace, which must be shown to the table.

After everyone has put in his or her ante, the dealer deals five cards facedown to each player.

Betting begins with the player to the left of the dealer. He may bet, check, or fold. Betting continues

clockwise around the table, and each player has the opportunity to call, raise, or fold. Some people play that it is necessary to have at least a pair of Jacks to open the betting in five-card draw. If the player closest to the dealer's left does not have a pair of Jacks or better, the betting moves clockwise around the table until a player with a pair of Jacks or better can open the betting.

After the first round of betting, all remaining players (those who did not fold) can draw up to three new cards from the deck (sometimes four cards are allowed; see front of card). The player discards the cards he does not want and is then dealt new cards from the top of the deck. Of course, if a player does not want any cards, he can "stand pat" and keep the hand he is holding.

Once all the players have received their new cards, the second round of betting begins. As in the first round, the player closest to the dealer's left opens, and the betting moves clockwise around the table. After all the bets have been placed, the players show their hands—the player with the best hand takes the pot. (For more on hands, see pages 10-12.)

Tips & Strategy :

- Traditionalists believe that to open the betting in five-card draw a player should have at least a four-card flush, four-card straight, or a high pair.

However, if betting is light and you are holding a small pair, a medium pair, or even two high cards, you might want to stay in for the next round. (A high pair is generally a pair of Jacks or higher; a pair of 7s, 8s, 9s or 10s would be considered a medium pair; and a pair of 6s or less is a small pair).

- If the betting is high in the opening round and you are not holding at least a pair, there is a good chance that at least one player has at least a high pair. This is particularly true with more players at the table. However, if players are betting high in the opening round, it indicates strength, regardless of the number of players. Your chances of drawing a hand to beat them are slim, so consider folding (or bluffing) rather than chasing cards in the hopes of improving your hand. You might get lucky on the draw, but, in the long run, you'll save a lot of money by getting out when you should.

- If you are dealt a strong hand—a high three of a kind or better—hold off on raising or opening with a large bet: You do not want to scare off any potential bettors. With a strong hand, play it cool in the opening round and just call bets. In some cases, a raise might work if another player has already raised the opening bet.

- However, if you have a high pair, consider making a fairly high bet. This is a strong hand but certainly

not unbeatable. By betting high you might drive out some players and improve your chances of winning the pot.

- It might seem obvious, but to improve your hand on the draw, you need something to draw to. So if you are holding a pair of Kings, keep them and draw three new cards. Players who keep their pair and draw three new cards have a 1 in 3.48 chance of improving their hand. (For more on the probabilities of improving your hand, see page 89–91.)

- In general, it is smarter to build on what you have, rather than chase a possible hand. For instance, if you are dealt 8-9-10-J-J, don't break up the pair of Jacks in the hopes of drawing to a straight.

- Drawing to a four-flush or a four-straight can pay off. However, going after an inside straight, or a three-straight (three cards in sequence) or three-flush (three suited cards) is risky at best. Smart players don't even try. Drawing to an inside straight (see Glossary, page 106) has very little chance of success and is a common novice mistake. Most professional players will tell you never draw to an inside straight.

- During the draw, keep a close eye on how many cards other players draw. By noting their draw, you will gain some insight into the strength of their hands. In general, if they draw three cards, they are probably holding a pair. If they draw two, they have three of a kind or are foolishly going after a straight or a flush. If they draw one card, they might have two pairs or they may be trying to draw a straight or flush. Players can also stand pat (not draw any cards). This means they are holding a good hand, perhaps a full house, straight, or flush. Or they may be bluffing.

- For bluffers, five-card draw allows two chances to ply their deceit: the betting and the draw. Players try to fool their opponents into thinking they have a better hand by standing pat or drawing just one or two cards or no cards at all and then raising in the second round of betting.

- Try and detect any tells in other players once they pick up their new cards. Did you pick up any reaction when they received their new cards? Do they seem a little too eager to start the second round of betting?

- Another strategic ploy in five-card draw is holding on to a "kicker." A kicker is an extra high card you keep when drawing to a pair. Thus, if you have a low pair, say a pair of 6s, you hold on to a high card in the hopes of getting a high pair to go along with your low pair.

- Holding on to kickers also throws off your oppo- nents. If you draw two cards to a low pair and a

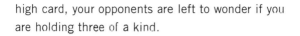

high card, your opponents are left to wonder if you are holding three of a kind.

- After the draw, pay attention to how players bet. If they bet aggressively or make a big raise, there is a good chance that they improved their hand (or they're bluffing). If they check the betting or bet modestly, they are probably unsure whether their hand is good enough to win and are playing it safe.

- By the second round, if you feel that your hand has a strong chance of winning, don't be afraid to bet aggressively. At this point, you want to maximize the pot and make your opponents "pay" to see your hand.

Sample Hand :

- -

OPENING DEAL:
- **PLAYER 1:**   6♦, K♦, 4♦, A♥, 5♦
- **PLAYER 2:**   K♠, 8♥, 7♥, 5♥, 6♠
- **PLAYER 3:**   4♠, 4♥, 2♣, 2♠, 10♣
- **PLAYER 4:**   Q♥, Q♠, 8♠, 9♦, 3♣
- **PLAYER 5:**   K♣, K♥, A♠, 9♠, 3♦
- **PLAYER 6:**   9♥, 8♣, 6♥, 4♣, 2♦

Betting: Stakes are $1/$2.This kind of denomination is common at a low-level casino table. The game is played with anyone able to open the betting.

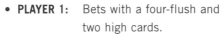

- **PLAYER 1:** Bets with a four-flush and two high cards.
- **PLAYER 2:** Calls with an open-ended four-straight.
- **PLAYER 3:** Raises with two pairs.
- **PLAYER 4:** Calls with a pair of Queens.
- **PLAYER 5:** Calls with a pair of Kings.
- **PLAYER 6:** Folds with nothing.
- **PLAYER 1:** Calls the raise.
- **PLAYER 2:** Calls the raise.

DRAW:
- **PLAYER 1:** Discards the A♥ in the hopes of drawing a flush.
- **PLAYER 2:** Discards K♠ in the hopes of drawing a straight.
- **PLAYER 3:** Discards the 10♣ in the hopes of getting a full house. (However, most players will assume he is going for a flush or a straight.)
- **PLAYER 4:** Draws to the pair of Queens.
- **PLAYER 5:** Draws two cards to the pair of Kings and holds on to the A♠ as the kicker. Some might dispute this logic, since holding on to kickers makes more sense with a low pair.

AFTER THE DRAW:
- **PLAYER 1:** He got it! He drew the J♦ and has a flush: 6♦, K♦, 4♦, 5♦, J♦

- **PLAYER 2:** Got the straight:
  8♥, 7♥, 5♥, 6♠, 9♣

- **PLAYER 3:** No help.
  4♠, 4♥, 2♣, 2♠, 7♣

- **PLAYER 4:** No help.
  Q♥, Q♠, 8♦, 7♠, 3♠

- **PLAYER 5:** No help.
  K♣, K♥, A♠, Q♣, 3♥

Betting:
- **PLAYER 1:** Bets big with a strong hand.
- **PLAYER 2:** Calls the bet.
- **PLAYER 3:** Folds. Since both player 1 and player 2 drew one card, and both bet, he figures at least one of them has a better hand than two low pairs.
- **PLAYER 4:** Folds with a pair.
- **PLAYER 5:** Folds with a pair.

WINNER:
- **PLAYER 1 with a flush.**

FIVE-CARD STUD
If It's Good Enough for Steve McQueen

PLAYERS: 2 to 10.

CARDS: Four up cards, one "hole" card.

BETTING: There are four rounds and betting picks up in the later rounds.

WHAT TO WATCH FOR: Do your first two cards offer any hope for building a strong hand? Look at your opponents' up cards: Do they have cards that you need to improve your hand? What type of hands are they going for?

WHAT WINS: Winning hands tend to be low. High pairs or better usually take the pot.

With the uncertainty of that one hidden card (hole card), five-card stud has its own mystique. It is, after all, the game that Steve McQueen and Edward G. Robinson played in *The Cincinnati Kid*. With four cards showing, each player has a fairly solid basis upon which to judge the hands of his or her opponents. However, the hole card can make or break a hand and is often what the game and betting hinge on. To improve your chances of taking the pot, pay close attention to your opponents' up cards, remember what cards have been folded, and assess your chances for improving your hand as the game goes along.

The game begins with the dealer giving each player one card facedown. The dealer then deals each player one up card.

The player with the highest card showing starts the betting. The betting then moves clockwise around the table. Some open the betting the opposite way and have the player with the lowest card open the betting in the first round. The dealer must decide who opens prior to dealing the cards.

After the first round of betting is completed, the dealer deals another up card to each player. At this point, and for the remainder of the game, the player with the highest-ranking hand showing opens the betting, followed by the person on his left, and then moving clockwise around the table.

Once the second round of betting is finished, the dealer gives each remaining player another up card. At this point, all remaining players have three up cards and a hole card. Another round of betting commences, followed by the fourth and final up card being dealt, followed by betting. After all players have placed their bets, everyone shows their cards with the highest hand taking the pot.

In *The Cincinnati Kid's* climactic scene, Lancey Howard's [Edward G. Robinson] straight flush beats the Kid's [Steve McQueen] full house. It makes for great drama, but in reality, it would probably never happen.

Tips & Strategy :

- Five-card stud often rewards skill since smart players carefully watch what other players have and
  assess the chances of improving their hands. Also,
  try and remember what cards have been folded.
  (For more about assessing your chances for improving your hand, see page 91 on "outs.")

- A key thing to remember about five-card stud (and
  poker in general): Don't be afraid to fold early, even
  after the first round, if you have mediocre cards.
  While it's true that occasionally you will catch some
  good cards and improve your weak opening cards,
  in the long run, it's better to play the percentages
  and fold early.

- There is a variety of opinions about what players
  should stay in the game after being dealt their first
  two cards. Conventionally, players will fold after the
  first two cards if they do not have a high pair, two
  high cards, or an Ace or King high. If you have less
  than this, only stay in if the other up cards can't
  beat you or the betting is light and it is worth staying in to get another card.

- If you are dealt a low pair with the first two cards,
  be wary of staying in the game too long, particularly
  if you do not get a three of a kind with the third
  card. Also, if another player has a high card show-

ing and is betting aggressively, he might have a
high pair

- If you are dealt two suited cards and are thinking
about chasing a flush, proceed with caution. Going
for a flush in five-card stud is risky even after
having three or four suited cards. It is particularly
dangerous if your suited cards are low. (If one of
the cards is high, you still have a chance of at least
getting a high pair.) If you try for the flush, you
must pay attention to whether any of the up cards
in your opponents' hands are of the same suit,
which would reduce your chance of completing
the flush.

- If the cards you need to improve your hand are
visible in your opponents' hands, they are "dead"
to you. When you are trying to complete a straight,
look around the table to see if another player is
holding cards you could use; if they are, your
chances are greatly reduced. For instance, if after
the first three cards you have J-10-9, and you
notice that two opponents are showing 8s and
another has a Queen, your chances of filling that
straight are in jeopardy. In five-card stud, it is
crucial to continually assess and reassess your
chances of improving your hand.

- You can also get a sense of whether your
opponents' hands can be improved by looking at

their up cards. For instance, if you have three 2s (two showing and one in the hole) and an opponent is showing two Aces, look around the table and see if any other Aces are exposed. If other Aces are exposed, your probability of winning is greater.

- Don't be self-centered. While you might stay in the hopes of trying to improve your hand, remember your opponents are doing the same thing. For instance, let's say an opponent's up card is a King and you have a 7 as your up card and a 10 in the hole. If you stay in with the hopes of getting a pair, keep in mind that your opponent has the same odds of pairing his King. If your opponent begins raising or stepping up his betting in later rounds, he might have gotten that pair, so proceed cautiously. In stud games, always keep an eye on the other cards on the table. Knowing what is on the table allows you to reassess the odds. Using our example from above, if two other players are also dealt a King, the chances of anyone getting a pair of Kings are dramatically reduced.

- Don't play a hand that you know is lower than your opponents' hand. If the up cards in an opponent's hand are better than yours, fold, even if you are holding a pair or better. You might get lucky and improve your hand enough to win, but as the expression goes, don't bet on it.

- In most stud games, the betting gets stiffer as you get into the later rounds. If you are still in by the third round, you must consider whether the amount of the pot is large enough to warrant staying in with an uncertain hand. One way to think about this is that by placing a bet you are essentially "buying" another card. So, if your opponent makes a bet, you must assess whether it is worth calling his bet to get another card in the hopes of improving your hand. Again, this should only be done after weighing the various factors, such as what your opponents are showing and whether the cards you need are still "live."

- Use your hole card to your advantage. In general having a "split" pair is better than having an exposed pair. For instance, if you have an Ace in the hole (now you know where the expression comes from) and one showing, you are at a distinct advantage compared to having both Aces showing. Your opponents will be left to guess whether your high betting means you've got an Ace hidden or you're bluffing.

- In general, if you've got a "cinch" hand by the final round (though remember nothing is 100 percent certain), bet aggressively.

Sample Hand

Betting: Stakes $1/$2. This kind of denomination is common in low-stakes casino poker.

OPENING DEAL:

	Hole cards	Up cards
• **PLAYER 1:**	9♠	6♠
• **PLAYER 2:**	6♣	A♥
• **PLAYER 3:**	K♦	8♥
• **PLAYER 4:**	10♠	10♥
• **PLAYER 5:**	8♠	J♥
• **PLAYER 6:**	2♦	K♠
• **PLAYER 7:**	6♥	6♦

Betting:

- **PLAYER 2:** Ace high opens the betting with $1.
- **PLAYER 3:** Folds, noticing the King in Player 6's hand.
- **PLAYER 4:** Calls the bet with a pair of 10s, a good hand, but does not want to disclose his pair by raising.
- **PLAYER 5:** Folds.
- **PLAYER 6:** Calls, hoping to pair up his King.
- **PLAYER 7:** Calls with a pair of 6s, hoping to catch a break in the next round.
- **PLAYER 1:** Calls, figuring the betting is still low and he'll pay to see another card.

SECOND ROUND:

	Hole cards	Up cards
• **PLAYER 1:**	9♠	6♠, 2♣
• **PLAYER 2:**	6♣	A♥, 5♦
• **PLAYER 4:**	10♥	10♠, 5♣
• **PLAYER 6:**	K♠	2♦, A♠
• **PLAYER 7:**	6♥	6♦, 7♦

Betting:

- **PLAYER 1:** Not receiving much help, he checks.
- **PLAYER 2:** Not receiving much help, he checks.
- **PLAYER 4:** Bets $1. Still has a fairly strong hand with a pair of 10s and assumes Player 2 does not have much, since he checked.
- **PLAYER 6:** Calls with two high cards.
- **PLAYER 7:** Calls with the pair of sixes.
- **PLAYER 1:** Folds.
- **PLAYER 2:** Folds.

THIRD ROUND:

	Hole cards	Up cards
• **PLAYER 4:**	10♥	10♠, 5♣, 7♣
• **PLAYER 6:**	K♠	2♦, A♠, K♣
• **PLAYER 7:**	6♥	6♦, 7♦, 3♣

Betting:

- **PLAYER 6:** Bets $2 with a pair of Kings. He knows that his King pair can beat the table.

- **PLAYER 7:**   Folds, worried that his pair of 6s will not hold up.

- **PLAYER 4:**   With A♠ & K♣ showing in his opponent's hand, considers folding, but stays in with a pair of 10s.

FOURTH AND FINAL ROUND:

	Hole cards	Up cards
• **PLAYER 4:**	10♥	10♠, 5♣, 7♣, 9♦
• **PLAYER 6:**	K♠	2♦, A♠, K♣, 10♣

Betting:

- **PLAYER 6:**   Knows he has won, since no matter what Player 4's hole card is, he can not beat a pair of Kings. He bets $2.
- **PLAYER 4:**   Knows he is either beaten or Player 6 is bluffing with the Ace high. Hoping Player 6 is bluffing, Player 4 calls the bet.

WINNER:
Player 6 with a pair of Kings.

SEVEN-CARD STUD
Where the Pots Get Bigger

PLAYERS: 2 to 7.
CARDS: Seven total: three in the hole, four up cards.
BETTING: Five rounds. Intensifies in the later rounds.
WHAT TO WATCH FOR: Is your hand improving? Are your opponents' hands? Are the cards you need still "live"?
WHAT WINS: Usually two pair or better wins, with one of the pairs being a high pair.

As the name suggests, seven-card stud is a stud game with seven cards, in which four are up and three are in the hole. Each player selects five of his or her cards to make the best hand (the other two cards are irrelevant to the outcome of the game). With several rounds of betting, pots can get pretty big pretty quickly, and betting intensifies in the late rounds. Seven-card stud is a fun game and hands take longer to develop, which entices many players to stay in longer. The three hole cards provide suspense and opportunities for bluffing. Seven-card stud is also demanding—good players keep a close eye on their opponents' up cards, notice how their opponents' betting changes with each new card, and remember what cards have been folded. Note: Many people play seven-card stud as a Hi-low game, which adds yet another element of strategy to the game.

In the first round, the dealer gives each player one card facedown, starting with the player on his left. He continues with a second down card and finishes by dealing a third card up. This up card is sometimes referred to as the door card.

Generally, the player with the highest up card starts the betting (some play with the low card opening the first round). If two or more players share the highest-ranking up card, the person closest to the dealer's left begins the betting. This first round, sometimes known as "third street" (each player has three cards), ends after each player has either placed his or her bet or folded. Next comes "fourth street"; at this point, all remaining players get another up card, followed by another round of betting.

There are two more rounds of up cards and betting (fifth street and sixth street), followed by the final card, which is dealt facedown to all remaining play-ers. At this point, all remaining players have four up cards and three cards in the hole. After the final round of betting, the players show their hands and the one with the best hand takes the pot.

Tips & Strategy :

- Seven-card stud allows a little more flexibility than five-card stud, but you still need to be careful about staying in too long with a questionable hand. Many experienced poker players will tell you that the first round is crucial—they will fold if, in the first round, they are not dealt at least a high pair, a pair in the hole, a pair with a high card, a three-flush, or a three-straight.

- If you are initially dealt a low pair, and your hand does not improve with the next two cards, you should fold. Of course, there is some flexibility here depending on the betting and other players' cards. However, if you don't have much of anything after the first four cards, you should consider folding.

- In the first round, if you are dealt a three-straight or a three-flush, stay in. But if you do not improve to a four-card straight or flush after two more up cards, fold. However, if after five cards you have a four-card straight or flush, draw the sixth and seventh card unless you think another player has you beat, or many of the cards you need are dead.

- If you are dealt three of a kind (a.k.a. trips) in the opening round, count your blessings. However, be careful about how you bet. Three of a kind might be strong enough to win the hand without any improvement, so you don't want to drive anyone out too quickly. In the first couple of rounds keep the betting moderate: Call bets and don't raise. If your hand still looks like a winner once the high streets roll around (fifth to seventh), start raising the stakes, since the remaining players are less likely to give up on their investment in the pot.

- If you are playing at a tight table and your two hole cards are a high pair, your early round of betting should be conservative. If you have a pair of Aces in the hole and a 4 showing and start with a big bet, people will fold, figuring you have something buried.

- If you are playing at a loose table and you are dealt a high pair, you can be a bit more aggressive with your betting. Players will be more willing to stick around in seven-card stud since hands take longer to develop. And don't worry if some players fold—it will decrease the number of people competing for the pot.

- If you begin with a high split pair in the early rounds, many experienced players will tell you to raise the betting. At this point, your hand is strong but not unbeatable and you'll need to catch another good card or two. You want to get rid of some players while it is cheap to do so. (The betting gets much higher in the later rounds, and people who have made it that far are less likely to fold.) With opening high pairs, always consider if another player has a higher door card, in which case you should moderate your betting because he or she might have a pair that can beat you.

- As in five-card stud, keep a close eye on what your opponents' up cards are and try to remember what cards have been folded. If you know what cards are dead to you and what "outs" you have remaining, you are in a better position to know if your hand can be improved. Likewise, by having a sense of what cards are on the table, you can get a better

read on your opponents' hands. Your ability to make an educated guess becomes crucial as you enter the later and higher-betting rounds.

- The betting gets serious in the last three rounds of seven-card stud. Assess your hand and your opponents' hands; if you feel like you've got the winning hand, bet aggressively in the last two or three rounds. If you've made it this far but are unsure if your hand has what it takes to win, you have two options. You can fold, of course, or decide whether drawing another card is worth the money.

- Use scare cards to your advantage. These are exposed cards that improve your hand or set up a potentially stronger hand. For instance, if you receive a suited Queen on fourth street to go with your King, your opponents will now worry you have a straight or a flush. Likewise, keep an eye on your opponents' high cards.

- With three hole cards, two of which are dealt in the first round, bluffers are emboldened in seven-card stud. However, don't just bluff willy-nilly. It is necessary that your exposed cards have potential. For instance, if you have three-suited cards (three cards of the same suit) exposed and are betting heavily, your opponents might think you have a flush. Also, if you are bluffing in seven-card stud, your betting should be consistent.

Sample Hand :

OPENING DEAL:

	Hole cards	Up card
• **PLAYER 1:**	Q◆, 5♥	A♠
• **PLAYER 2:**	Q♥, 4♣	6♠
• **PLAYER 3:**	2◆, 3◆	J♥
• **PLAYER 4:**	A♠, 10♣	2♥
• **PLAYER 5:**	K♥, 4◆	6◆
• **PLAYER 6:**	6♥, 5♠	7♣
• **PLAYER 7:**	10♠, 7♠	Q♠

Betting:	Stakes $1/$2.
• **PLAYER 1:**	Bets with two high cards.
• **PLAYER 2:**	Folds, having unsuited cards and noticing the exposed Queen and Ace.
• **PLAYER 3:**	Folds.
• **PLAYER 4:**	Calls with suited Ace.
• **PLAYER 5:**	Calls with two diamonds and a King, in the hopes something will develop.
• **PLAYER 6:**	Calls with a three-straight.
• **PLAYER 7:**	Stays in with a three-flush.

SECOND ROUND:

	Hole cards	Up cards
• **PLAYER 1:**	Q◆, 5♥	A♠, 3♠
• **PLAYER 4:**	A♣, 10♣	2♥, 9♣
• **PLAYER 5:**	K♥, 4◆	6◆, 6♣
• **PLAYER 6:**	6♥, 5♠	7♣, 8◆
• **PLAYER 7:**	10♠, 7♠	Q♠, 7♥

Betting:

- **PLAYER 5:** Bets with a pair of 6s and a King.
- **PLAYER 6:** Bets with a four-straight.
- **PLAYER 7:** Bets with three-flush.
- **PLAYER 1:** Bets with a suited Ace.
- **PLAYER 4:** Bets with three clubs and an Ace.

THIRD ROUND:

	Hole cards	Up cards
• **PLAYER 1:**	Q♦, 5♥	A♠, 3♠, J♦
• **PLAYER 4:**	A♣, 10♣	2♥, 9♣, 10♥
• **PLAYER 5:**	K♥, 4♦	6♦, 6♣, 9♦
• **PLAYER 6:**	6♥, 5♠	7♣, 8♦, A♥
• **PLAYER 7:**	10♠, 7♠	Q♠, 7♥, Q♣

Betting:

- **PLAYER 7:** Still not seeing much on the table. Bets with two pairs of Queens over 7s.
- **PLAYER 1:** Folds, having noticed another Ace and three diamonds on the table, thus recognizing the low probability of improving his hand.
- **PLAYER 4:** Stays in with pair of 10s, hoping to catch a two-pair.
- **PLAYER 5:** Folds, figuring his pair of 6s won't hold.
- **PLAYER 6:** Stays in with four-straight.

FOURTH ROUND:

	Hole cards	Up cards
• PLAYER 4:	A♣, 10♣	2♥, 9♣, 10♥, 9♥
• PLAYER 6:	6♥, 5♠	7♣, 8♦, A♥, 4♥
• PLAYER 7:	10♠, 7♠	Q♠, 7♥, Q♣, 8♣

Betting:

- **PLAYER 7:** Bets high with two pair.
- **PLAYER 4:** Folds, worried that Player 7 has at least two pair Queen-high.
- **PLAYER 6:** Got the straight and raises.
- **PLAYER 7:** Calls.

FIFTH ROUND:

	Hole cards	Up cards
• PLAYER 6:	6♥, 5♠, 8♥	7♣, 8♦, A♥, 4♥
• PLAYER 7:	10♠, 7♠, 3♥	Q♠, 7♥, Q♣, 8♣

Betting:

- **PLAYER 7:** No help, but bets, either failing to recognize the strength potential or assuming that Player 6 is bluffing.
- **PLAYER 6:** Feels confident with straight and raises.
- **PLAYER 7:** Calls.

WINNER:
Player 6 with a straight.

TEXAS HOLD 'EM
Today's Glamour Game

PLAYERS: Two to twenty-three (Optimal amount is seven to nine).

CARDS: Each player gets two pocket cards, plus five community cards in the "widow" (see below).

BETTING: Four rounds with betting doubling in last two rounds; play with ante or blinds.

WHAT TO WATCH FOR: Make sure you can build on your pocket cards. Pay attention to how players bet after the flop.

WHAT WINS: Usually a high pair or better.

Many hardcore poker players consider Texas Hold 'em the game of games. It has had a surge of popularity in recent years as the official game of the World Series of Poker and many other tournaments. Home poker players should be aware that the tournament games are usually played as "no limit" games and have very different betting strategies.

Texas Hold 'em is a community card game in which you try to construct the best five-card hand from three of the five community cards (known as the "widow") plus the two cards dealt to you. (It is possible that only one of your pocket cards will be used, say to make a pair with a card from the widow, and the other will function as the kicker.) The two cards dealt to each player are placed facedown or in the hole or pocket; the five community cards are

placed facedown in the middle of the table.

After each player is dealt his or her two hole cards and the community cards are laid facedown, the first round of betting begins with the player to the dealer's left. That person begins the bet each time. You are not allowed to check in the first betting round; you must either bet or fold.

Once the first round of betting is done, three community cards are turned over—this is called the flop. After the flop, another round of betting takes place. The fourth community card is then flipped—the turn, or fourth street and players bet again. However, if you want to stay in for this round and the last (the "river" or fifth street), you must bet double the minimum bet. For instance, if $1 is the minimum bet for the game, you must bet at least $2 on the turn and on the river. After the river card is flipped over, there is one last betting round and then the showdown. It is sometimes possible that a tie will occur, in which case the pot is split.

At the casinos, the betting in Texas Hold 'em usually starts with "blinds" rather than antes. However, if you are at home, and playing several different games in an evening, it is recommended that you use antes in Hold 'em (for more on blinds, see page 87). With antes, everyone contributes to the pot before the deal, but with blinds, it is only the two people closest to the dealer's left. So if you are playing several different games, it is better to keep the ante consistent, so everyone has anted the same amount in the end.

Tips & Strategy :

- In Hold 'em you definitely need to know when to "fold 'em." If you are dealt pocket cards that have no chance, it's in your best interest to either fold right away or, if the bet is low enough, stay in one round to see the flop. An example of a hand that offers little hope would be low unconnected (two cards not in sequence) and unsuited cards, say the 2 of clubs and an 8 of diamonds. Immediately you see that there is no possibility for a straight or a flush, and the cards are very low.

- If you are new to Hold 'em and are playing with more experienced players, you should get out early if you have weak pocket cards, or if you are uncertain about your hand's worth. Otherwise, your losses will add up quickly. Since Hold 'em games tend to be fast, it's okay to fold often; you won't have a lot of down time.

- The best kind of hole cards you can get are high cards (ten or higher) that are paired (ex.: Q-Q), connected (ex.: J-Q), the same suit, or offer more than one "out" or way to win the hand (such as cards that could contribute to a straight or a flush). Ideal hole cards would be a high pair.

- Remember, you are sharing several cards with the table, and the hand can be decided by just one of

your pocket cards. This means that you've got to have cards that can knock out other hands in more than one way. A pair of low pocket cards, such as 5s, will probably not take you very far, since if there is any card higher than a 5 in the widow, it is likely that someone will have a higher pair than yours.

- Your position at the table is crucial in Hold 'em. If you are dealt weak pocket cards, and you are in early position (one of the first players to bet), you should probably get out right away. However, if you are in late position (one of the last to bet), you have the benefit of seeing how many people fold and how others bet. With a late position you can get away with playing a less-than-perfect hand and perhaps employ your bluffing skills, particularly if the previous bettors don't appear overly aggressive. For instance, if you are dealt a 5-8 and the betting is light, you can figure that other players probably also have weak pocket cards, and a low pair, two pair, or low straight might take the pot.

- Sometimes your pocket cards and the flop will immediately reveal a strong hand, or a potentially strong hand, such as three or more suited cards, a high pair, or better. The direction you should take will be clear—you should stay in and bet according-ly, taking into consideration the cards and your opponents' betting.

- The problem with "over cards": Over cards are pocket cards that are higher than any cards in the widow. Let's say the flop is generally lousy for you, and the whole table, because it doesn't offer many potential hands. Should you stay in with your high cards and hope that you get a match to pair one of your pocket cards? Or should you see if you can win simply by having the high card? It can be a hard call. If you're in early position, you should check and wait to see if anyone makes an aggressive bet. If you're in late position, you can see how others have played and then decide whether to call the bet. If it looks like the other players don't have much, you can take a chance and stay in, but if the bets are aggressive, you should probably fold.

- Most hands are defined on the flop, so if you have stayed in, you should start to be more aggressive. By deciding to stay in for the turn and then the river, you should have a hand that is a true contender. If you don't, there is not much point in continuing, since it's going to cost you to stay in. Most players who stay in for the later rounds have got something—you need to be able to beat them or at least be confident that you can bluff them into folding.

- After the turn, and especially after the river, the game may be down to two or three players and you should be using all of your poker skills at this point. Ask yourself some questions. What is the likelihood that your opponent has the particular card to win? Is your opponent exhibiting tells? How well do you know this opponent? How has this player been betting—aggressively by raising and re-raising, or just calling? Examine the widow carefully and make sure you are seeing all of the possible winning hands. If there is the possibility that you are both going for a flush, what is the probability that you will have the higher flush?

Sample Hand :

Betting: Stakes $1/$2.

Pocket Cards

- **PLAYER 1:** 2♣, 8♥
- **PLAYER 2:** K♥, 3♣
- **PLAYER 3:** Q♥, Q♣
- **PLAYER 4:** 7♥, 8♣
- **PLAYER 5:** A♠, J♦
- **PLAYER 6:** 5♥, 6♦
- **PLAYER 7:** K♦, A♣

FIRST ROUND (remember there is no checking allowed in first round):

- **PLAYER 1:** Folds. The cards are too low, unsuited, and can't make a straight.
- **PLAYER 2:** Bets $1 to see the flop, although with a 3 kicker it's not very promising.
- **PLAYER 3:** Raises $1. The Queens are a very strong starting hand.

- **PLAYER 4:** Folds. Although the 7 and 8 have a straight potential, the betting from Player 3 scares him off.
- **PLAYER 5:** Calls the bet with two high cards.
- **PLAYER 6:** Folds for the same reason as Player 4.
- **PLAYER 7:** Calls the bet and raises another $1.
- **PLAYER 2:** Folds. The 3 kicker is too low to contend with the betting.
- **PLAYER 3:** Calls the raise.
- **PLAYER 5:** Calls. He's a little worried that Player 3 and Player 7 have a high pair, but he likes Jack with the Ace kicker.

THE FLOP: J♠, 3♠, 10♦

- **PLAYER 3:** Bets $1. Still feeling good with the Queens since there is no higher card in the widow.
- **PLAYER 5:** Calls. He now has a pair of Jacks with an Ace kicker. As far as he knows, he has the high pair since there is nothing higher in the widow; still Player 3 and Player 7 could have a higher pair.
- **PLAYER 7:** Raises $1. He likes his King-Ace, there is the potential straight, and he sees the Jacks as the highest possible pair. He has also been playing aggressively and he wants to maintain his presence.
- **PLAYER 3:** Calls the raise. He still likes his

Queens but is slightly worried. Player 7 bet aggressively from the beginning, so it's possible he has a pair of Jacks in the hole, but Player 3 knows Player 7 may also have a King-Ace. If Player 7 holds a pair of Jacks, his three of a kind would win, but if he only has a pair of Jacks, Player 3's Queens will beat it.

- **PLAYER 5:** Calls the raise. Slightly worried that picture cards will appear on the turn.

THE TURN: J♠, 3♠, 10♦, 2♣ Remember, the bet doubles in the last two rounds.

- **PLAYER 3:** Bets $2. Feeling good with the Queens since the 2♣ helped no one.
- **PLAYER 5:** Calls the bet since nothing has changed.
- **PLAYER 7:** Calls the bet for the same reason as Player 5.

THE RIVER: J♠, 3♠, 10♦, 2♣, Q♦

- **PLAYER 3:** Checks. Knows that if Player 7 bets aggressively, then he's probably got the straight.
- **PLAYER 5:** Folds. Knows that his pair of Jacks is most likely beaten with the Queen.
- **PLAYER 7:** Bets $2.
- **PLAYER 3:** Calls.

WINNER: Player 7 with a straight.

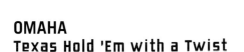

OMAHA
Texas Hold 'Em with a Twist

PLAYERS: Two to eleven (ideally, seven to nine).
CARDS: Each player has four pocket cards; there are five community cards.
BETTING: Ante plus four rounds with bets doubling at fourth street.
WHAT TO WATCH FOR: Pairs and suited cards in the widow. Low cards if you are playing Hi-low.
WHAT WINS: Relatively high hands, straight or better. When playing Hi-low, your highest card should be no higher than an 8.

Omaha is played like Texas Hold 'em except each player is dealt four cards in the hole instead of two. The real trick is to remember you must use two cards and only two cards from your hand and three from the community hand.

The first round of betting begins with the player to the left of the dealer. As in Texas Hold 'em, players cannot check in the first round. After the first round of betting, the dealer turns over the first three community cards—the flop—and there is another betting round. After the fourth community card is exposed, known as fourth street or the turn, the third betting round takes place. As in Hold 'em, the bet now doubles. As in Hold 'em, the opening bet must be at least twice the minimum bet.

Finally, the last common card—fifth street or the

river—is flipped over, and there is one final bet. If you are new to Omaha, it may take some time to figure out what you have. Because you have four cards in your hand, you may have more than one good hand.

A fun twist to Omaha is to play it as a Hi-low game. In fact, most Omaha games are played as Hi-Low. There are some differences between regular Hi-Low and Omaha Hi-Low. If you are going for the low hand in Omaha, you cannot have a card higher than an eight. For instance, you could have 2, 4, 6, 7, 8 as your low, but not 2, 4, 6, 7, 9. As in other Hi-low games, there is the possibility of going for both the high and low hands. In Omaha you can try for both using the four cards in your hand. If your pocket cards were A♠, 2♥, K♣, K♥ you have two very good low cards and two good high cards. Unlike regular Omaha, if the widow produces the cards you need, you can use your two low cards and the two high cards separately to form two potentially winning hands. (Remember, if you are trying to win both the low and the high, you must win both to claim any of the pot. Therefore, it is crucial that you make sure you have the best of both hands.) When playing Omaha it is not uncommon to have ties, especially low ties. In these cases, the winner of the high hand gets half, and the two tied low hands split the other half.

Tips & Strategy :

• The widow in Omaha, combined with the fact that
players have four cards to choose from, provides a
wealth of information. For instance, if you see a pair
in the widow, you should assume that at least one
player has a full house. Because more than one
player can have the full house, you should make sure
that you can beat it with higher cards. For instance,
if two 7s are showing, and someone is betting fairly
aggressively, you should assume that he or she is
using that pair toward a full house. It is quite possible that you are also using the two /s towards a full
house. However, if the other community cards are a
King, 2, and 4, and the other part of your full house
is the 4s in your pocket, you have to figure out
whether your opponent has the King by estimating the
probability and reading the signs he is giving you.

• Some of the same strategy from Hold 'em can be
applied to Omaha, but, because you get four cards
instead of two, there are many more opportunities
for success. This is especially true if you are playing Hi-low.

• If you are dealt low pocket cards, it's worth your while
to see the flop, especially if you have suited, or connected, cards or even a low pair. A low pair might lead you
to a full house, but low pairs alone are still low and will
probably be beaten. Even though you can only use two

of the cards in your hand, by having four you are open to more possibilities than in Hold 'em.

- If there is a potential for a flush or a straight in the widow, it is very likely that someone will have it. If there are three diamonds showing in the widow, you must remember that because each player has four pocket cards, there is a strong likelihood that someone is holding two diamonds. Straights are not as common as flushes in Omaha, but beware, especially if there is a potential high straight in the works. If the flop produces three cards of the same suit, then everyone should be a little scared. But if a pair turns up, either on the turn or the river, it is more than likely that your flush is now no longer a threat because of the potential for a full house.

- In general, because there are more ways to win, you can stay in longer with lower cards in Omaha. However, it is still in your best interest to have high cards because it is likely that several players may have almost identical hands and the absolute highest hand will obviously win.

- Although more people will pay to see the flop in Omaha, it is a good idea, once you have seen the flop, to determine as quickly as possible if the cards are there to create a winning hand. If you don't see strong potentials such as pairs, same suits, or connected cards, you may want to get out before the

turn. The temptation will be stronger than in Hold 'em to stay in longer, since the four pocket cards offer more possibilities. However, as you play more often, you will quickly be able to see a strong starting hand. For instance, if you see a pair in the widow, but it does not have any immediate links to your pocket cards, it is probably not going to do you much good. Remember, a pair showing usually is helping someone at the table.

- If you are playing Omaha Hi-low, and there are unsuited and unconnected low cards in the widow, someone most likely has a good low hand. If the highest low card in the widow is a 5, be very careful; someone might be building a very strong low hand.

- In Omaha Hi-low, the hands that raise are usually going after the high hand, since it is much easier to predict. The low hand is sometimes so uncertain that it may not be clear until the river card whether you've made a successful low hand. Because players with the low hand may be betting more passively, it may be hard to read what they are up to.

- A good Omaha player will not make speculative bets. Since you get more pocket cards, it is very likely that you can construct a good hand, and bluffing will not help as much. If you stay in, you should be confident that you have the best hand, since it is likely that those who have stayed in really do have something worth playing for.

Sample Hand : OMAHA HI-LOW

PLAYING 1, 2, 3, 4, 6 as the best low
BET: $1/$2

POCKET CARDS:
- **PLAYER 1:** 2♥, 6♦, 9♦, J♥
- **PLAYER 2:** Q♦, Q♥, 8♠, 7♦
- **PLAYER 3:** 2♣, 4♥, 5♦, 10♠
- **PLAYER 4:** K♥, 2♠, J♦, 10♥
- **PLAYER 5:** 4♦, 5♥, 2♦, 7♥

FIRST BETTING ROUND (remember, no checking):

- **PLAYER 1:** Bets $1. He is not thrilled with his low cards and worries that his hearts and diamonds are too low.
- **PLAYER 2:** Calls the bet. Although the pair of Queens looks good, he will probably fold if the Ace or King appears in the flop.
- **PLAYER 3:** Calls. Does not have the greatest low cards and is worried that someone has the Ace and 3.
- **PLAYER 4:** Calls. Feels good with the two high hearts. The low is not possible.
- **PLAYER 5:** Calls. This hand offers several possibilities, but he is worried about the medium-range cards he has.
- **THE FLOP:** A♠, 3♥, K♠

- **PLAYER 1:** Checks. Has a good low hand in

the works with his A-2-3-6.

- **PLAYER 2:** Checks. The flop produces the dreaded King and Ace. He will see how people bet.

- **PLAYER 3:** Bets $1. So far, he has a great low hand, but knows he needs the 6. Although he doesn't have it yet, he feels confident.

- **PLAYER 4:** Folds. The low is not an option. He's afraid of the Ace and doesn't have a two-pair option. If he had been checked, he would've called.

- **PLAYER 5:** Raises $1. He is in the last position, which is a great advantage, and, with a great low hand in the works, he decides to pick up the betting.

- **PLAYER 1:** Calls.
- **PLAYER 2:** Folds.
- **PLAYER 3:** Calls.

THE TURN: A♠, 3♥, K♠, 6♣

- **PLAYER 1:** Checks. Not happy that a 6 turned up since he now needs a 5 to get the low. He needs one more heart for the flush but knows that his Jack is weak.

- **PLAYER 3:** Bets $2. He's secured the perfect low.

- **PLAYER 5:** Raises $2. He has also secured the perfect low hand and now has four hearts.

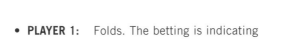

- **PLAYER 1:** Folds. The betting is indicating that the other guys have the low.
- **PLAYER 3:** Calls the raise and raises back.
- **PLAYER 5:** Calls the raise.

THE RIVER: A♠, 3♥, K♠, 6♣, 9♥

- **PLAYER 3:** Bets $2. Feeling extremely confident with his low hand.
- **PLAYER 5:** Calls. He now has the great low hand and the flush but he is worried that Player 3 has a higher pocket heart.

DECLARATION OF HIGH OR LOW:

- **PLAYER 3:** Going low.
- **PLAYER 5:** Going only low. He figures it's not worth the risk.

- Each player bets the $2.

- **WINNER:** The players split the pot since they both have the best low.

HI-LOW
Where a Terrible Hand Can Win You Money

In Hi-low, the players with the best hand (high) and worst hand (low) split the pot. The best hand is determined by standard poker rules (see card 4) the best low is A, 2, 3, 4, 6 or "6 down." (Some people play A, 2, 3, 4, 5 as the lowest hand.)

The winner of a low hand is usually determined by the lowest high card. If the highest cards are the same rank, move to the second-highest card and compare again. For instance, if Player 1 has 2, 3, 4, 7, 8, and Player 2 has 2, 3, 4, 6, 8, Player 2 wins because his 6 beats the 7.

In seven-card stud and other games with more than five cards, it's possible to declare both high and low. This is a more common occurrence when playing with wild cards. However, even without wild cards it is possible. For instance, if you are playing seven-card stud and your cards are A♥, 2♥, 3♥, 4♥, 5♥, 6♣, 8♦, you would have both a straight flush high hand and a 6 down (A, 2, 3, 4, 6) low hand.

Note: If a player declares both high and low, he must win both. If he loses either the high hand or the low hand, the player with the best remaining high hand splits the pot with the player with the best remaining low hand.

Hi-low is played the same way as other games with this exception: Prior to the last round of betting, or prior to the showdown (the dealer can decide), all players "declare" whether they are going for high or low. A common way of declaring is by placing chips in your hand. Players trying for the high hand put a chip in their hand, those going for low leave their hand empty, and those going for both put two chips in their hand. All players place a closed fist above the table and the dealer then asks all to open their fists and show whether they are going high or low. If a player is the only one to declare either high or low, he automatically wins half the pot. After the players declare, there is the showdown. (There are different variations on when and how to declare. Some declare sequentially, where the last player to raise is the first to declare. This method gives the last person to declare an advantage, because he knows what other players are declaring and can tailor his own declaration accordingly. Alternately, some players just lay down their cards after the final round of betting and let the cards speak.)

If the pot cannot be divided evenly, the player with the high hand takes the indivisible amount or it can be put toward the next game's pot.

Tips & Strategy :

- Hi-low can be tricky since you have to alter your way of thinking about things. In a sense, you want to develop hands that have the potential to be both low and high. Thus, having an Ace is a big advantage since it can be used as both a high and a low card.

- Anything below an 8 is considered strong for developing a low hand. As the game progresses, survey the table to see how many low cards are dead and assess your chances of improving your low hand.

- An ideal hand in the opening round of Hi-low is a three-card straight with all the cards being 8 or lower. This allows a player to pursue a low straight with the luxury of falling back on a low hand and vice versa. Keep in mind this factor makes straights much more common in Hi-low than in regular stud. Likewise, having three low-suited cards is also an excellent hand to be dealt, since it also gives you the opportunity for a flush and a low hand. Being able to pursue two different hands also keeps players in longer and betting tends to be higher.

- In seven-card Hi-low, low pairs in the early rounds are also valuable because if you get more low cards, you can split the pair(s) and pursue the low hand. You also have the potential to build off the pairs for a high hand (two pairs, three of a kind, or a full house.)

- Conventional wisdom says that having a high pair other than Aces is a somewhat lackluster hand to be dealt in the opening round of seven-card Hi-low. With straights being more common in Hi-low, even if the pair improves to a three of a kind, there is a chance it will lose.

- If you are confident that you have won either the high or the low hand, you should start raising and betting aggressively in the later rounds. For instance, if you sense you are the only one going for a high hand, start raising. The players with the low hands will continue to call in the hopes of making their hands.

- Like regular seven-card stud, it is important in Hi-low to examine your opponents' cards. Most of the time you can decipher whether or not someone is going for high or low, though surprises can occur. While surveying exposed cards, look at the highest card showing. Can you beat it as a low?

Sample Hand : SEVEN-CARD STUD HI-LOW

ROUND 1:

	Hole cards	Up cards
• PLAYER 1:	K♠, 5♣	K♥
• PLAYER 2:	6♠, 3♦	5♠
• PLAYER 3:	Q♦, 10♥	J♥
• PLAYER 4:	A♠, 6♥	3♠
• PLAYER 5:	8♠, 9♦	8♥
• PLAYER 6:	2♥, 9♠	Q♠
• PLAYER 7:	9♥, 10♣	5♦

Betting:
- **PLAYER 1:** Bets. Senses a good high hand with a pair of Kings.

- **PLAYER 2:** Calls. With 3, 5, 6 has a promising low hand.
- **PLAYER 3:** Calls. A solid beginning for a high hand with three connected high cards.
- **PLAYER 4:** Calls. A, 3, 6 is a good start to a low hand.
- **PLAYER 5:** Calls with a pair. Will fold quickly if hand does not improve with next card.
- **PLAYER 6:** Folds with little hope for either a low or high hand.
- **PLAYER 7:** Folds for same reason.

ROUND 2:

	Hole cards	Up cards
- **PLAYER 1:**	K♠, 5♣	K♥, 10♠
- **PLAYER 2:**	6♠, 3♦	5♠, 2♠
- **PLAYER 3:**	Q♦, 10♥	J♥, Q♥
- **PLAYER 4:**	A♠, 6♥	3♠, 3♣
- **PLAYER 5:**	8♠, 9♦	8♥, J♣

Betting:

- **PLAYER 1:** Checks. Still feels strong with King pair but wants to see what Player 2 and Player 3 do with two suited cards.
- **PLAYER 2:** Bets. He now can work for both the low hand and a flush with three spades.
- **PLAYER 3:** Calls. High hand now improved to a Queen pair and three-flush.
- **PLAYER 4:** Calls. Pair of 3s complicates things but still has a strong low hand.

- **PLAYER 5:** Folds.
- **PLAYER 1:** Calls.

ROUND 3:

	Hole cards	Up cards
• **PLAYER 1:**	K♠, 5♣	K♥, 10♠, 7♣
• **PLAYER 2:**	6♠, 3♦	5♠, 2♠, J♠
• **PLAYER 3:**	Q♦, 10♥	J♥, Q♥, 9♣
• **PLAYER 4:**	A♠, 6♥	3♠, 3♣, 6♦

Betting:

- **PLAYER 4:** Bets. Still working toward high (full house) and low hand.
- **PLAYER 1:** Folds. With little help and three spades in Player 2's hand, he's worried.
- **PLAYER 2:** Calls. Can still work for flush and low hand.
- **PLAYER 3:** Calls. Straight still good but worried about possible flush. in Player 2's hand.

ROUND 4:

	Hole cards	Up cards
• **PLAYER 2:**	6♠, 3♦	5♠, 2♠, J♠, 7♥
• **PLAYER 3:**	Q♦, 10♥	J♥, Q♥, 9♣, A♦
• **PLAYER 4:**	A♠, 6♥	3♠, 3♣, 6♦, 7♠

Betting:

- **PLAYER 4:** Checks. Wants to see how confident other players are.
- **PLAYER 2:** Bets. Has made a good low hand with 7 high and still has a shot at a flush.

- **PLAYER 3:** Calls. Looking at the up cards, feels he still has a chance at the high hand with a pair of Queens and possible straight.
- **PLAYER 4:** Calls.

ROUND 5:

	Hole cards	Up cards
• **PLAYER 2:**	6♠, 3♦, 4♦	5♠, 2♠, J♠, 7♥
• **PLAYER 3:**	Q♦, 10♥, Q♣	J♥, Q♥, 9♣, A♦
• **PLAYER 4:**	A♠, 6♥, 8♦	3♠, 3♣, 6♦, 7♠

Betting:
- **PLAYER 4:** Bets. Hopes 8 low will be enough.
- **PLAYER 2:** Raises. Looking to go for both high and low hands.
- **PLAYER 3:** Bets. Feels three Queens will take the high hand.
- **PLAYER 4:** Calls.

DECLARE:
- **PLAYER 2:** Both.
- **PLAYER 3:** High.
- **PLAYER 4:** Low.

SHOWDOWN:

Player 2's straight beats Player 3's three Queens; Player 2's 7 down beats Player 4's 8 down.

OTHER GAMES & THE POLITICS OF WILD CARDS

There are countless variations on the staple games of poker. Many of these games employ wild cards, in which a card can have any value. Hardcore poker players turn their nose up at wild cards, since they throw off the probabilities and change the nature of the game. However, for the rest of us, wild cards can be a fun way to spice things up a little. Keep in mind that wild cards affect the ranking of the hands: five of a kind is now the best hand. Not surprisingly, players stick around longer when wild cards are involved, pots tend to be bigger, and you might even see a royal straight flush lose to a five of a kind.

It is up to the dealer to decide what cards are wild in each game. He can essentially choose any card he likes to be wild. Common wild cards are deuces, threes, one-eyed Jacks, and the suicide Kings (King of hearts). Other games, such as Follow the Queen, have changing wild cards. And still another variation is to have the low card in the hole wild for each player. For instance, in seven-card stud, if you have a 5-9-10 in the hole, then all 5s in your hand, whether face up or down, are wild.

Follow the Queen

Follow the Queen is a fun variation on seven-card stud in which your hand can potentially change—and

change dramatically—with each new up card. Since the wild cards can change, it is difficult to have a strategy, but if you have a couple of Queens, you are in good shape. In Follow the Queen, Queens are always wild, whether exposed or in the hole. If a Queen is dealt faceup, then the next up card following the Queen is also wild. However, if the up card after that is a Queen, then the other wild card is replaced. For instance, let's say a Queen is dealt face up to Player 1, and then Player 2 gets a 3 up card. Queens and 3s, either up or down, are wild. But in the next round, Player 3 gets another Queen face up and Player 4 is dealt a 6 up card. Now 6s are wild, and 3s are just 3s.

With wild cards changing, a potentially winning hand in Follow the Queen can turn into a lousy one. Likewise, a hand going nowhere can be transformed into a full house or better. Unlike regular seven-card stud, in which the final card is dealt down, many people play that each person can opt to have his final card either up or down.

Roll Your Own

Roll Your Own is a variation on seven-card stud where each player decides what his hole cards are as the hand progresses.

The game begins with three cards being dealt face down to each player. The players then choose one of their three hole cards to reveal to the table. For instance, if a player is dealt a $10\heartsuit$-$10\diamondsuit$-$J\diamondsuit$, he can decide to keep the $10\diamondsuit$-$J\diamondsuit$ in the hole and expose the $10\heartsuit$. There is a round of betting and then another card is dealt face down. Once again, each player chooses one of his three down cards to expose. This sequence continues until each player has four up cards and two cards in the hole. The last card stays down as in regular seven-card stud.

An important decision in Roll Your Own is if, and when, to reveal your good cards. For instance, if dealt a pair, you can expose them, split them, or keep both hidden. Since players choose their hole cards, the game allows for bluffing and surprise endings.

Note: Roll Your Own is a fun game with plenty of suspense, but patience is required because it takes time for players to decide on their hole cards.

High Chicago

High Chicago is just like regular seven-card stud, except the person with the best hand must share the pot with the person with the highest spade in the hole (so if you have the Ace of spades showing, it does you no good). Like Hi-low, High Chicago is a declare game in which players declare whether they are going for the high hand, high spade in the hole, or both. If you are using chips, one chip is for high hand, no chip is for high spade, and two chips is for both.

Murder

Murder is a variation on High Chicago without any declaring. As in High Chicago, the high spade splits the pot with the best hand. However, the high spade can either be exposed or in the hole. Thus, in this game, if you have the Ace of spades, you are certain of having at least half the pot. However, if the Queen of spades appears among the up cards, the game is reset, the cards are collected, re-shuffled, and re-dealt. Sound crazy? It is, but it can be a lot of fun— unless you happen to have the Ace of spades when the Queen of spades shows up.

Basic Baseball

Basic Baseball is a seven-card stud game. Here are the fundamentals: 3s and 9s are always wild; if you are dealt a 4 faceup, you are eligible for an extra card facedown. (To help you remember the rules, think of the particulars of the game's namesake: There are three runs, nine innings, and four balls for a walk.) It is up to the dealer to decide if a fee will be charged for the extra card if you are dealt the 4; the dealer will also determine the amount. Some dealers may also make you pay to use the 3 as a wild card. However, the dealer usually charges for either the 3 or the 4, not both. If there is a charge, it works as follows: If you are dealt a 4 face up, you have the option to buy an extra card for the stated fee and add that amount to the pot. If the dealer chooses to charge you for the wild 3 face up, you must either add the fee to the pot or fold.

Night Baseball

Players receive seven cards face down—no peeking! As in Basic Baseball, 3s and 9s are wild and you can buy an extra card with a 4. To start, Player 1 turns over one of his cards and then opens the first round of betting. He may also pass. (The dealer must decide beforehand whether a passed play means the betting goes to the next player, or whether the next player simply begins to turn over his cards.) Player 2 then turns over his cards one at a time until he can beat the previous hand—he can then choose to bet or pass. If Player 2 chooses to bet, all players must bet or fold (many haven't seen their hand yet). After that betting round, Player 3 tries to beat the previous hand. If Player 3 can't beat the previous hand, he is out. Player 4 then bets or folds. This continues around the table until one player is left or everyone's cards are revealed. Some people play that if a player reveals a 3, he must pay a fee to stay in, or fold. It might seem there are endless betting rounds in this game, but it goes swiftly even after the first round.

Anaconda or "Pass the Trash"

In Anaconda every player is dealt seven cards. After an initial betting round, each player passes three of his cards to the player on the left. (One of Anaconda's cruel ironies is that in some cases you might have to break up a full house or a straight.) After receiving the new cards from the other player, each player selects five to make a hand and lays them face down in front of himself in the order in which he wants to reveal them. There is then another round of betting and then each player turns over one of his cards. The player to the dealer's left begins the betting. In each round, all players turn over a card and bet. After the fifth card is turned over, there is a winner—the highest hand.

The strategy in this game lies in the laying out of the cards and the betting. Some players reveal their strengths immediately and others let their hands develop slowly. In many cases, the game hinges on that final card. For instance, if you have a straight, and you've revealed 10, J, Q, K, your opponents will have to guess whether you are holding a 9 or Ace to fill your straight. You should also try to remember what you passed to your opponent and what cards have already been exposed—this will give you a better idea of what your opponents are holding.

Spit in the Ocean

Spit in the Ocean is a variation of five-card draw. Every player is dealt four cards face down instead of the normal five. The fifth card is dealt face up on the table and can be used by all the players. After one round of betting, starting with the player on the dealer's left, each player can draw up to two cards from the deck. After the draw, there is a second and final round of betting, followed by the showdown.

Twin Beds

Twin Beds is a combination of Draw, Spit in the Ocean, and Community games that can be played with three to ten people. Every player is dealt four cards face down. Then two rows of five cards each are dealt face down. There is a round of betting and then the dealer turns over one card from each row followed by another round of betting. This process continues until all the cards are turned over. However, the last card to be turned up from each row is wild, so if a 2 shows up in the last card, all 2s are now wild. Players may use their own cards plus up to five cards from one and only one of the rows to make the best hand; they cannot use cards from both rows to help their hand.

Cincinnati

In Cincinnati each player is dealt five cards (four is also an option) and five community cards are placed face down on the table. The common hand is revealed one card at a time followed by a betting round after each card is exposed. Players construct their best hand out of all ten cards.

Ohio

Ohio is played the same as Cincinnati except for a fun twist based on a wild card. The lowest-ranking card of the five community cards is wild. Unless you are a super math whiz you probably will not know what the wild card will be until the very end. If you are the dealer, make sure you declare whether Aces will be high or low before you begin.

For many games there are subtle variations. For instance, all games can be played where the low hand instead of the high hand wins. Instead of playing five- or seven-card stud, you can play six-card stud, in which the final card is dealt down, giving each player two hole cards and four up cards.

Guts

Beware—this game can cost you some money. To start, everyone antes and then each player is dealt two cards. After examining your hand, you declare whether you are in or out. If you don't feel you can win (winning hands are the single highest card or, better, the highest pair), you declare you're out and withdraw until the next hand. Those who are in reveal their hands and the winner takes the pot. Here's where it can start to get pricey—all players who were in and lost must match what was originally in the pot! So if the original pot was a dollar, then the losers must each put in a dollar. This then means that the next round will open with a $3 pot. The cards are reshuffled and dealt again to the whole table and the process continues— and this time any losers must each contribute $3 to match the pot. The game ends when only one person calls in and collects the pot. If you're lucky, you can win some big bucks playing Guts. But if you're reckless, you can potentially lose a chunk of your bank. (This game is best with four to seven players.)

Whiskey Poker

There is not a lot of money involved in Whiskey Poker but it can be a fun break in between more hardcore games. Whiskey Poker is a community card game in which each player receives five cards. Five additional cards are then dealt face down in the middle. Everyone bets. The player to the left of the dealer has the option of trading in her whole hand for the widow. If the player makes the trade, then the exchanged hand is placed face up in the middle of the table. However, if this player declines to exchange, the option is offered to the next player and so on. If no one trades his or her hand with the widow, then it is turned face up by the dealer. Now the first player can trade one to five cards with the widow or pass. Players cannot pass more than twice. When a player feels he has a winning hand during his turn, he knocks on the table. Everyone to his left will have one more opportunity to exchange cards with the widow. When the round returns to the "knocker," a second and final bet occurs.

Betting Strategy
GETTING THE MOST BANG FOR YOUR BUCK

Each game has its different nuances when it comes to betting. However, here are some general tips on betting that can help you in any game:

- In the long run, knowing when not to bet is one of the most important skills to have in poker. It is also important to make the pots you win count through strategic betting. If you have a good hand, your strategy should be to build the pot as much as possible with aggressive bets and raising in the later rounds. The trick is not to bet so high in the early rounds that you force players to fold and therefore lessen the pot.

- As with everything in poker, observe the betting habits of your opponents. Within a game, if a player starts betting high and then starts checking or betting less aggressively, the hand he was hoping for might not have materialized.

- If you are playing at a loose table, it will be harder to steal pots (winning pots by bluffing), but you can expect bigger payoffs when you win.

- Be decisive in your betting. No one likes to wait as you hesitate with your bet. Betting quickly also gives your opponents less time to read your habits.

- If you are playing at a tight table, an aggressive bet

will win you some small pots in the early rounds. However, be careful that you are not caught in a bluff and forced to pay up with a weak hand.

- If you have a not-so-stellar hand, aggressive betting can help you steal some pots. If the betting has been light in the early rounds, your opponents are signaling weak hands. If you come in with a big bet, you might force the other players to fold and come away with the pot. It might not be a big pot, but you can take it with very little in your hand.

- Checking can be a great strategic tool, especially if you are uncertain of the relative strength of your hand. If you have a less-than-perfect hand, you can see if the other players come out betting aggressively or passively. If a lot of people fold and the other players who stayed in were passive, then you may have a chance. However, if the bets were aggressive and you get the sense that you can be beaten, you should probably fold when the betting comes back around to you.

Bluffing
STAYING STRAIGHT-FACED WHEN
YOUR INTENTIONS ARE CROOKED

- Don't be afraid to bluff. Even the most honest souls should bluff every so often, just to keep opponents a

bit off balance. If you never bluff and only bet with strong cards, players will know you only stick around with a good hand. In this case, when you have a strong hand they may fold early and ruin your chances of taking a massive pot. Admittedly, you might have to lose a round or two by having someone call your bluff, but in the long run, it's worth it.

- Conversely, don't press your luck. Bluffing should be part of your poker arsenal, but you should use it wisely. Many players get a bit too enamored with their skills of deception and lose a lot of pots by having their bluffs called.

- If your bluffing forces everyone else to fold and you win the pot, you don't have to show your hand— just quietly take your winnings. In fact, it's best to keep your opponents guessing about your hand. However, when you've bluffed and lost a few times, it might be a good idea once or twice to let your opponents know that you were bluffing. This tells your opponents that you aren't afraid to bluff and in later rounds will make them wonder if your high betting is a sign of a great hand or a bluff.

- Each game calls for different types of bluffing. In five-card draw, you can bluff through your betting and the number of cards you choose to draw. In stud games, be aware of what your hand looks like to other players. For instance, if you are betting heavily

in a seven-card stud game in which you're showing 7-8-9-10 and have 2-3-Q in the hole, your opponents might assume that you have a Jack or 6 to complete the straight. If you are betting heavily and consistently raising, they might very well call your bluff.

- In stud games, look at the up cards to assess whether the big bettor actually has a good hand or is just bluffing. Also try to notice any "tells" (see page 94) the bettor might be revealing.

- One of the ironies of poker is that it is easier to bluff experienced players than novices. Knowing when to fold and learning self-discipline in poker takes time—new players are much more likely to call all bets.

- Don't bluff against lots of players, particularly in the later rounds of a stud or community game. Chances are that at least one of those players will be holding something good.

Betting Odds and Ends
BLIND BETS, BETTING BLINDLY, AND CHECKING BETS

- Blinds are a common feature in Hold 'em and are a way to get the betting going in a game. Blinds, as the name implies, are blind bets placed by the first two players to the dealer's left before the players even look at their pocket cards. They function the same way as antes by making players invest in the game. The "small blind", is placed by the player directly to the dealer's left and is usually smaller than the established minimum bet, but it can be the same. The player seated two places to the left of the dealer places the "big blind," which is usually double the amount of the small blind. The betting then starts with the player to the left of the big blind and he or she can simply call the big blind, raise, or fold. Once the bet returns to the players who threw the blinds, they have the option of raising, which is known as a "live blind."

- Sometimes emotions play a role in betting. Players who have been losing might start making wild bets to recoup their losses. Likewise, players who have been winning tend to get a little sloppy, figuring they're already ahead and can afford to lose a little. If you can pick up on these shifts and avoid falling into the same traps, you stand to win a few extra pots.

- There has always been some debate as to whether check-raising should be allowed in home poker games. Some feel it creates a less-than-friendly atmosphere. Check-raising is when a player, usually in an early position at the table, checks and then raises when the bet returns to him. Because checking usually indicates that you are uncertain of the

value of your hand, some consider check-raising a mean-spirited attempt at bluffing to get more cash out of your fellow players. However, other players contend that check-raising is a perfectly legitimate poker tactic and its use should never be questioned.

- When playing poker, particularly if you're at a casino, bet whatever you're comfortable with. You should go into any poker situation with confidence but recognize the cards might not go your way. Always think about how much money you are willing to lose. Set limits for yourself and be prepared to walk away from a table if things are not working out. Losing streaks are part of poker, but you don't want to find yourself in a situation where you are desperate to win back your losses. This will only lead to bad betting and unsound poker decisions.

The Mathematics of Poker

Poker is a game of probability, not certainty (otherwise, there would be no betting). There are many books out there that dissect the mathematics of poker. While you can probably leave your slide rule and calculator at home, to be a successful player you should have an appreciation of the numbers.

Every deck of fifty-two cards has 2,598,960 possible five-card poker hands. Below are the odds of being dealt the following hands with the first five cards.

TYPE OF HAND	QTY IN DECK	ODDS AGAINST
Royal Flush	4	649,739:1
Straight Flush	40	64,973:1
4 of a Kind	624	4,164:1
Full House	3,744	693:1
Flush	5,108	508:1
Straight	10,200	254:1
3 of a Kind	54,912	46:1
2 Pairs	123,552	20:1
1 Pair	1,098,240	1.25:1
No Pair	1,302,540	Evens

Before trying to fill that inside straight (it will happen only once in eleven tries), you should have a good idea of what your chances are. Below are the odds against improving your hand in draw; they can also help you think about your odds in stud games as well:

CARDS KEPT:	CARDS DRAWN:	IMPROVED HANDS:	ODDS AGAINST:
1 Pair	3	2 Pairs	5.25:1
1 Pair	3	3 of a Kind	8:1
1 Pair	3	Full House	97:1
1 Pair	3	4 of a Kind	359:1
1 Pair	3	Any Improvement	2.5:1
2 Pairs	1	Full House	11:1
3 of a Kind	2	Full House	15.5:1
3 of a Kind	2	4 of a Kind	22.5:1
4-Straight (open-ended)	1	Straight	5:1

CARDS KEPT:	CARDS DRAWN:	IMPROVED HANDS:	ODDS AGAINST:
4-Straight (inside)	1	Straight	11:1
Four-flush	1	Flush	4.5:1
Three-flush	2	Flush	23:1
Two-flush	3	Flush	96:1

The Ins and Outs of Outs and More on Poker Odds

By calculating your "outs"—what cards you need to win—and combining them with some basic probability, you are well equipped to decide when to fold and when to stay in.

First, you need to remember that there are fifty-two cards in the deck. Easy so far, right? Next you need to count how many cards you actually see. For instance, if you are playing Hold 'em, you see the two cards in your hand and the cards in the flop, turn, or river. In stud games, you will see your hole card(s) and everyone's up cards. So in Hold 'em, for example, if you see a total of six cards (two in your hand and four in the widow), then you subtract that amount from fifty-two and get forty-six—this is the number of cards you have not seen.

The next steps involve figuring out what your potential winning hands are, what cards will make these hands, and how many more opportunities you have to get them.

In many cases you will have several outs—more than one way you can win. Let's say in Hold 'em your pocket hand is 6♦-7♦. The flop shows 5♦-8♦-6♠. So at the beginning you see that you have a pair of 6s and a four-flush hand. In order to start thinking about what a winning hand is, you must assess what is the best possible hand showing. In this example with a widow of 5♦-6♠-8♦, someone may have a straight or be working on a flush, so unless you luck out, and two more 6s appear in the widow, the pair is of little value to you. However, you are in good shape because you only need one diamond. And, if you are really lucky, you might get the 9 of diamonds and get a straight flush. You could also make straight with the 5♦-6♠-8♦ already showing, but someone else may have the straight already, so you probably want to focus on drawing the flush. Admittedly, it is a lot to think about, but as you play more and more, these types of assessments will become second nature. To break down the odds even further, go to the next card.

AS A REMINDER, OUR TEXAS HOLD 'EM HAND HAS 6♦-7♦ IN THE POCKET AND 5♦-6♠-8♦ IN THE WIDOW. ON THE TURN YOU WOULD LIKE TO SEE:

1. One more diamond for the flush. There are thirteen diamonds in the deck and you see four of them = nine outs.

2. A 9 of diamonds for the straight flush. There is only one 9 of diamonds in the deck = one out.

NOW YOU APPLY THE OUTS TO FIGURE PROBABILITY AND ODDS: For the flush you have seen five cards, forty-seven cards remain, and there are still nine diamonds out there that can help you. Since nine out of the forty-seven will get you your flush, you have approximately a 19 percent chance of getting your flush on the turn. However, with two chances (the turn and the river), at this point, you can estimate the odds by doubling, so figure you have about a 38 percent chance of getting your flush.

For the straight flush you have seen five cards, forty-seven remain, one card can help you, and you have two more chances of getting the 9♦.

PROBABILITY: 1 in 47 or approximately 2 percent. Two chances would make it 4 percent.

If the turn reveals a K♥, your outs have not changed. However, you now only have one more shot at getting another diamond, so if other players are betting high, be careful.

Learning how to calculate outs can and should be applied to stud games as well. Since there are more cards out there, it is a little trickier. In stud games look at other players' exposed cards, remember what cards have been folded, and count how many cards are left that can help you to calculate your odds.

When calculating odds, you must remember that it is a tool to help you get a better sense of your chances; it cannot tell you whether or not you will win. Obviously, you do not know what cards your opponents have in the hole, so your calculation of the odds is only based on what you see. Apply your assessment of your outs with other information at your disposal, particularly how players are betting. All of this is to say that calculating outs will definitely make you a better poker player—but it's no guarantee. There's always that thing called luck.

Tells THE PSYCHOLOGY OF POKER

Being a good poker player requires a variety of skills, not the least of which is being a good psychologist. Tells are the habits and quirks that let players know when their opponent is bluffing or holding a strong hand. Tells reveal different things for different players. Some people play with their chips when they are bluffing and others when they have a good hand. As you play more often, you will become a better interpreter of tells.

Try to notice any tells that you might be exposing yourself. It's harder to pick up on your own behavior, but remember that just as you are watching other players, other players are watching you.

HERE ARE SOME EXAMPLES OF CLASSIC TELLS:

- **CHUCKING CHIPS:** If a player throws the chips into the pot with an exaggerated motion, he is probably putting on an act to appear confident.

- **HIDING THE GOODS:** Often when players are cover-

ing or "guarding" their cards, it means they've got something good.

- **CAN'T TAKE MY EYES OFF YOU:** By staring at their cards, players try to deceive other players into thinking they've got a great hand.

- **SIT UP STRAIGHT:** If a player has good posture, it might just mean a good upbringing. But players subconsciously sit up straight or lean forward with strong cards.

- **AND THE OSCAR GOES TO . . . :** Overacting, particularly among novice players, is a common way to try to fool other players. Someone with a good hand might act unusually quiet, while someone with a bad hand might act overly elated. However, if the person seems genuinely happy, he or she probably has good cards. With a strong hand, players tend to relax and let their true emotions show—you just have to know what to look for.

- **"ARE YOU LOOKING AT ME?":** Actually, if a player is looking away from the table, he might be feigning indifference and have a good hand. Players with good hands often don't like to call attention to themselves.

- **PUTTING YOUR MONEY WHERE YOUR MOUTH ISN'T:** Occasionally players with good hands will subconsciously cover their mouths when betting.

- **FEELING STRESSED?:** Anxiety can come out in poker through shaky hands, a high voice, and even an expanding chest.

- **"NEVER COUNT YOUR MONEY WHEN YOU'RE SITTING AT THE TABLE":** People who start fingering their chips are often planning their attack. This could be a sign of anxiousness.

- **DON'T PEEK:** Players who habitually look at their hole cards are often still working to improve their hand.

- **CHIP ARCHITECTURE AND THE FRANK LLOYD WRIGHTS OF POKER:** While it is hardly a science, aggressive players tend to have loose stacks of disorganized chips while conservative players often keep their stacks nice and tidy.

"The main reason people fail to accomplish as much as they could—in poker and in life—is *they don't play their best game always.*"

—Mike Caro,
Caro's Fundamental Secrets of Winning Poker

Casino Poker
TAKING YOUR GAME TO THE BIG TIME

Playing poker in the casino is vastly different from the casual poker game at home. Poker in the casino can be fun, but if you are not careful, it can also be quite costly. Here are some things to be aware of before booking your tickets to Las Vegas or Atlantic City:

- First, poker is the only game in the casino where you are not playing against the house—you are playing with strangers. Be aware that some of these strangers might be pros; they will know you are a rookie before you even sit down. Obviously, not everyone is going to be a shark, particularly at the low-limit table, where there will be plenty of people who enjoy poker but only play occasionally at casinos. But before sitting down at a table, walk around the casino and try and find a table where you think you might be comfortable.

- A good place to start would be a low-limit table where the minimum bet is $1 or $2 and the maximum bet is $2 or $4. Because the stakes are low, you will probably be playing with people of similar skill level. Also, the betting will be light enough that you won't feel intimidated.

- If you thought table etiquette was important at home, it is doubly important in the casino. Things like playing out of turn, moving your cards from the table, and mishandling chips can have serious consequences. Not only will your fellow players have zero tolerance for your misbehavior, but your mistakes could lead to disqualification of your hand. It is quite all right for you to mention to the dealer that you're a rookie. It is the dealer's role to let you know when you should move and to remind you of rules. Don't worry about exposing yourself as a novice; it will most likely be apparent anyhow.

- Ever wonder how the casinos make money from poker since the gamblers are not playing against the house? The casinos can charge an "admission fee" by requiring you to pay to sit down; they can also take a percentage of the winnings. If you go to the casino with a set amount of money to gamble with, just remember that not all of that money will be for making bets. This fee is something to think about if you plan to play lots of hands; it will add up.

Online Poker
OR, BLUFFING WITH MOUSE IN HAND

In recent years, online poker has exploded in popularity. It is estimated that between 2002 and 2003, partici-pation increased by a whopping 600 percent. In fact, Chris Moneymaker, a recent winner of the World Series of Poker, honed his skills at online tables.

There are literally dozens if not hundreds of Web sites where you can play poker (Hold 'em and seven-card stud are the most popular varieties). In the past few years, the improved security of Web sites has made online gambling much safer. (However, as with anything on the Web, if something looks fishy, do not provide any crucial information.)

To start playing, you usually need to download the necessary free software; provide a credit card number to open an account, which you can cash out at any time; and create a login name (this will be the name you use at the table). Most sites should provide some information about themselves, which you should investigate before submitting a credit card number.

Once you enter a site you will see a lobby listing various games at different betting levels. After choosing a game, you will be taken to a simulated poker table, complete with cards, chips, and other players. Most sites have a dealer that will prompt you to bet.

If you are new to online poker, most sites have tables where you can play for free. It's a good idea to play a few practice hands at the free tables to get a sense of the pace and where to click to fold, raise, bet, etc.

Once you are ready to start playing for money, check out what games are available. Many sites offer a wealth of statistics about the various tables, including average pot size, hands, players per hour, and the average wait to get on a table.

Obviously, the biggest difference about playing

online against other people is you can't see them—no need to worry about keeping a poker face. However, you should still apply all your normal poker skills to online playing. You should also observe the same rules of etiquette, in particular, make your bets promptly.

There are also countless Web sites devoted to all things poker. For players of all skill levels, the Internet is an invaluable resource for finding about everything from rules and strategy to tournaments and casinos. Many of these sites have articles from profes sional poker players. For the beginning player, whether at home or online, the following sites might be useful:

www.online-poker.com, www.virtual-poker.net, www.thepokerforum.com, www.homepoker.com, www.playwinningpoker.com

Poker Books
AFTER YOU'VE READ THE CARDS...

Poker has inspired countless books on strategy as well as more literary/journalistic efforts. Here's a small sampling of some notable titles:

- *The Literary Side: Poets (and Others) At the Poker Table,* **by A. Alvarez**

- *The Biggest Game in Town,* **by A. Alvarez**
  What do poker and Sylvia Plath have in common?
  A. Alvarez. The English poet, critic, and one-time

friend of Sylvia Plath looks at high-stakes poker in Las Vegas. *The Biggest Game in Town* is a cult classic.

- *A Friendly Game of Poker: 52 Takes On the Neighborhood Game,* **edited by Jake Austen**
  A collection of writings on poker with essays from Nick Tosches, Ira Glass, Richard Meltzer, and others.

- *Poker Nation: A High-Stakes, Low-Life Adventure Into the Heart of a Gambling Country,* **by Andy Bellin**
  A look at the world of professional poker with plenty of helpful advice, including a section on odds.

- *Super/System*, **by Doyle Brunson, et al.**
  When you're ready for your post-graduate degree in poker... This comprehensive look at the odds and probabilities of poker revolutionized the game when it was published in 1978.

- *Caro's Fundamental Secrets of Winning Poker,* **by Mike Caro**
  Caro is definitely a distinctive voice in poker. This book is excellent for beginners and more advanced players. Lots of strategy and statistics to improve your game. Caro has also written an excellent book on tells.

- *Poker for Dummies*, **by Richard D. Harroch & Lou Krieger**
  The Basics.

- *Big Deal: A Year As a Professional Poker Player,* **by Anthony Holden**
  Holden takes a break from his life as a biographer and critic to pursue poker professionally, culminating in a seat at the World Series of Poker.

- *Positively Fifth Street: Murderers, Cheetahs, and Binion's World Series of Poker,* **by James McManus**
  McManus's account of the murder trial of Ted Binion and his own run at the World Series of Poker.

- *Amarillo Slim In a World Full of Fat People: The Memoirs of the Greatest Gambler Who Ever Lived,* **by Amarillo Slim Preston**
  The title alone is almost worth buying the book. However, you will also find entertaining anecdotes and advice from a poker legend and winner of the World Series of Poker.

- *Scarne's Guide to Modern Poker,* **by John Scarne**
  Provides rules and some of the essential poker playing tips.

- *The Theory of Poker,* **by David Sklansky**
  This work and others by Sklansky are considered must-haves for the serious poker player. Sklansky breaks down and explains a variety of strategies.

- *Thursday Night Poker: How to Understand, Enjoy, and Win,* **by Peter O. Steiner**
  An excellent guide for the intermediate player.

- *The Education of a Poker Player,*
  by Herbert Yardley
  A classic. This is definitely old school, but very helpful and fun to read.

Glossary : GET TO KNOW THE TERMS

ACES UP: a hand with two pairs in which the high pair is Aces. You can use this expression for other cards. For example, if you had a pair of Kings and a pair of 4s, you could say, "Two pair, King high" or "Two pair, Kings over 4."

ADVERTISE: to deliberately bluff and expose yourself as a loose player.

ALL-IN: to bet all your remaining chips. A more common occurrence in high-stakes poker, particularly in tournaments.

ANTE: an amount, decided before playing begins, that each player puts in the pot before the game begins.

BAD BEAT: when you play the correct odds but lose to a lucky hand. It happens.

BET INTO: to bet before someone whose hand appears better or who made a high bet the previous round.

BIG BLIND: a compulsory ante made by the person sitting two away from the dealer's left. Commonly used in Hold 'em. See **Blind.**

BLIND: compulsory ante made by the player on the dealer's left. Again, common in Hold 'em. Also, a bet made before looking at the cards. See **Big Blind.**

BLUFF: to bet big with a poor hand to fool opponents into folding.

BOARD, ON THE: The cards that are exposed to all players. The center cards in community games such as Omaha and Hold ' em or the up cards in a stud game.

BOAT, OR FULL BOAT: a full house.

BULLET: an ace.

BUMP: to raise. "I'll see your $10 and bump you another $10."

BUST: a hand that failed to materialize into anything good.

BUY-IN: the minimum money needed to sit in on a game.

CALL: to match a previous bet.

CHASE: to look for one specific card, or cards, in the hopes of improving your hand.

CHECK-RAISE: to check with a strong hand in the hopes of raising when the betting comes back around. A controversial strategy. Also known as "sandbagging."

CINCH: a hand that cannot lose. Also known as a "lock" or "nuts."

COMMUNITY GAMES: games such as Hold 'em, Omaha, or Cincinnati, where players share a number of cards from the board.

CONNECTED CARDS: cards that are in consecutive order, for instance 4-5 or Q-K.

DEALER'S CHOICE: playing with a rotating dealer who chooses the game.

FIFTH STREET: in Hold 'em or Omaha, the fifth and final card to be turned over. In seven-card stud, the fifth card dealt. See **River**.

FLOP: in Hold 'em or Omaha, the first three cards on the board to be exposed.

FOLD: to quit a hand.

FOUR-FLUSH OR FOUR-STRAIGHT: a hand with either four cards of the same suit or four cards in sequence. Until these hands are "filled" with a fifth card, they are worthless.

FOURTH STREET: in community poker, the fourth card to be exposed. In stud games, the fourth card dealt. See **Turn.**

FOUR TITS: a pair of Queens. Also known as a "Siegfried and Roy."

HI-LOW: In Hi-low games, the highest and lowest hands split the pot.

HOLE CARDS: concealed cards in stud or community games such as Hold 'em or Omaha.

IN: if you call all bets, you're still "in" a hand.

INSIDE STRAIGHT: a four-straight where you need one specific card to fill a straight. For instance, 9-10-Q-K. Chasing an inside straight can be risky. See **Open-ended straight**.

KICKER: another card, usually high, that strengthens your hand but does not contribute to a pair or better. A hand of 10-10-A-6-4 would be a "pair of 10s with an Ace kicker."

LIMIT POKER: a game in which maximum bet limits are established.

LOCK: see **Cinch**.

LOOSE: a loose player is someone who bets recklessly in defiance of the odds. See **Tight**.

MAKE: to make the deck means to shuffle.

MUCK: where discarded or folded cards go.

NUTS: see **Cinch**.

OPEN: to make the first bet in a game.

OPEN-ENDED STRAIGHT: four cards in sequence that can become a straight with two different cards on either end. For instance, 8-9-10-J (a 7 or Q would fill the straight). See **Inside straight**.

POT ODDS: the ratio of money in the pot to the money you must put in to stay in the hand. Calculating pot odds is a good way to figure if it is worth staying in a hand.

RAISE: to increase the amount of the previous bet. "I'll see your $5 and raise you another $10." See **Bump**.

RIVER: the final card exposed in a community game. See **Fifth Street.**

SANDBAGGING: see **Check-raise.**

SEE: to see a bet means to call or match the previous.

SHOWDOWN: the point at which players expose their hands to determine the winner.

SIEGFRIED AND ROY: see **Four Tits.**

STAND PAT: to not take any cards from the deck in a draw game.

STEAL: taking the pot with a poor hand by bluffing your opponents into folding.

STREAK: a run of good or bad cards.

STUD: a game in which each player is dealt a card or cards facedown followed by up cards.

SUITED: cards of the same suit. if you are dealt the Ace and King of spades you have "Ace-King" suited.

TELL: a mannerism that gives away a player's hand.

TIGHT: a conservative player who usually only bets when his hand is strong. See **Loose.**

TRIPS: three of a kind.

TURN: in a community game, the fourth card turned over. See **Fourth Street**.

UNSUITED: cards of different suits.

UP CARD: a card exposed to the table.

WIRED: a pair in the hole. For example, in a seven-card stud game, if your two down cards are Kings, you've got "Kings wired."